NATIVE AMERICAN NATIONS

Algonquin

F.A. BIRD

CONTENT CONSULTANT: MKOMOSE

**Checkerboard
Library**

An Imprint of Abdo Publishing
abdobooks.com

ABDOBOOKS.COM

Published by Abdo Publishing, a division of ABDO, PO Box 398166, Minneapolis, Minnesota 55439.
Copyright © 2022 by Abdo Consulting Group, Inc. International copyrights reserved in all countries.
No part of this book may be reproduced in any form without written permission from the publisher.
Checkerboard Library™ is a trademark and logo of Abdo Publishing.

Printed in the United States of America, North Mankato, Minnesota
102021
012022

THIS BOOK CONTAINS
RECYCLED MATERIALS

Design and Production: Mighty Media, Inc.
Editor: Liz Salzmann
Cover Photograph: Francis Vachon/Alamy Photo
Interior Photographs: Ad_hominem/Shutterstock Images, p. 7; Akshay-PhotOvation/Shutterstock
    Images, p. 21; Andrew Rivett/Flickr, p. 15; Bildagentur Zoonar GmbH/Shutterstock Images, p. 5;
    Christoph Ulański/Flickr, p. 17; Cortomaltais/Wikimedia Commons, p. 9; Francis Vachon/Alamy
    Photo, pp. 19, 23; German Vizulis/Shutterstock Images, p. 27; Mark Byer/Shutterstock Images,
    p. 11; P199/Wikimedia Commons, p. 25; wdeon/Shutterstock Images, p. 29; WilliamSherman/
    iStockphoto, p. 13

Library of Congress Control Number: 2021943040

Publisher's Cataloging-in-Publication Data
Names: Bird, F.A., author.
Title: Algonquin / by F.A. Bird
Description: Minneapolis, Minnesota : Abdo Publishing, 2022 | Series: Native American nations | Includes
    online resources and index.
Identifiers: ISBN 9781532197147 (lib. bdg.) | ISBN 9781098219277 (ebook)
Subjects: LCSH: Algonquin Indians--Juvenile literature. | Indians of North America--Juvenile literature. |
    Indigenous peoples--Social life and customs--Juvenile literature. | Cultural anthropology--Juvenile
    literature.
Classification: DDC 973.0497--dc23

Contents

CHAPTER 1

Homelands

The Algonquin (al-gon-kwin) are members of the Anishinabek (a-nish-naw-bek) Nation. The Anishinabek people include the Algonquin, Ojibwa or Chippewa, Delaware, Mississauga, Odawa, and Potawatomi.

The Algonquin have lived in North America for thousands of years. Anishinabek **elders** teach that the Algonquin have lived in North America since time began.

The Algonquin settled along the St. Lawrence River and the Ottawa River. These rivers flow through the Canadian **provinces** of Ontario and Quebec. The area is a land of rocks and shallow soil. It is covered with forests of birch, maple, poplar, oak, and many kinds of evergreen trees. Everywhere, there are pure lakes and rivers.

Part of the Algonquin homeland is now Algonquin Provincial Park in Ontario, Canada.

CHAPTER 2

Society

The Algonquin people divided into **bands**. These bands were usually led by the women. During the summer, the bands camped together.

In the winter, the bands divided into much smaller groups. Often, just one or two family **clans** made a small winter camp in their hunting grounds.

The Algonquin did some farming. But in some areas, the summer was too short to grow many crops. The Algonquin also got food by hunting, fishing, and gathering. Preserving the family hunting grounds was important. Families **inherited** the right to hunt and fish there.

THE ALGONQUIN HOMELANDS

BRITISH COLUMBIA
ALBERTA
SASKATCHEWAN
MANITOBA
WASHINGTON
OREGON
IDAHO
MONTANA
NORTH DAKOTA
MINNESOTA
WYOMING
SOUTH DAKOTA
WISCONSIN
MICHIGAN
NEVADA
UTAH
NEBRASKA
IOWA
CALIFORNIA
COLORADO
KANSAS
ILLINOIS
INDIANA
OHIO
MISSOURI
ARIZONA
NEW MEXICO
OKLAHOMA
ARKANSAS
KENTUCKY
TENNESSEE
ALASKA
TEXAS
LOUISIANA
MISSISSIPPI
ALABAMA
GEORGIA
FLORIDA
NORTH CAROLINA
SOUTH CAROLINA
VIRGINIA
WEST VIRGINIA
PENNSYLVANIA
NEW YORK
MAINE
VERMONT
NEW HAMPSHIRE
MASSACHUSETTS
RHODE ISLAND
CONNECTICUT
NEW JERSEY
DELAWARE
MARYLAND
WASHINGTON, DC
ONTARIO
QUEBEC
PRINCE EDWARD ISLAND
NEW BRUNSWICK
NOVA SCOTIA
HAWAII

Lake Superior
Lake Huron
Lake Michigan
Lake Ontario
Lake Erie
Ottawa River
St. Lawrence River

THE ALGONQUIN HOMELANDS

N
W E
S

CHAPTER 3

Homes

The Anishinabek lived in different types of wigwams (WIHG-wahm). Thin tree branches or **saplings** were placed in a circle to form the wigwam's frame. The branches were tied together at the top to make either a dome or a cone shape.

The outside of the wigwam was made of strips of birch bark or animal hides sewn to thin branches. This was then wrapped around the wigwam's frame. A hole at the top let out the smoke from the fire inside.

In the winter, the Anishinabek covered the wigwam floor with spruce branches. The branches were covered with animal skins to make a warm floor. When the Anishinabek moved, they took the outside coverings and floor coverings with them. They left the frame behind.

Most birch bark wigwams were about ten feet (3 m) wide and eight to ten feet (2.4 to 3 m) tall.

CHAPTER 4

Food

The Algonquin gathered wild rice, berries, and sap from maple trees. Sometimes, they planted crops such as corn, beans, and squash. Commonly hunted animals included moose, caribou, deer, porcupine, beaver, and bear.

The Algonquin fished in many different ways. At night, they put a bright torch in the front of a canoe. Then, they speared the fish that were attracted to the light. In the winter, they cut holes in the lake ice. Then, they fished with hooks and spears. The Algonquin also used large traps called "fish fences" to catch fish.

The term *moose* comes from the Algonquin word *moosewa*. It means "eater of twigs."

CHAPTER 5

Clothing

The Algonquin wore deerskin **tunics**. Women's tunics were longer than men's, ending below the knees. In the summer, the Algonquin wore sleeveless tunics. The men wore **breechcloths** in the summer and tight leggings in the winter. Everyone wore moccasins.

In the winter, the Algonquin wore large robes made of animal skins over their tunics. They also used the robes as sleeping bags. And they wore mittens, hoods, and fur caps.

An Algonquin woman prepares a deer skin for use in making clothing.

CHAPTER 6

Crafts

The Algonquin used birch bark for many things. In June and July, birch bark could be easily peeled off birch trees in large, unbroken sheets. Then, the bark was separated into paper-thin sheets.

The Algonquin made cups by rolling the bark into cone shapes and sewing the seams together with plant fibers. They also made boxes and dishes out of birch bark. Boxes, dishes, and cups were often decorated with porcupine **quills**. The quills were colored with natural dyes. Large rolls of birch bark were used to make cradles. The cradles were lined with moss.

Birch bark was also used to build canoes. Birchbark canoes were strong but light. Two men could carry a 25-foot (7.6 m) canoe 4 miles (6.4 km) without resting. The canoe could hold 3,000 pounds (1,361 kg) of **cargo** and ten people.

Algonquin canoe makers soaked sheets of birch bark in water until it was soft enough to bend around the canoe frame.

CHAPTER 7

Family

All Algonquin are members of a clan. Each clan is named after an animal, such as the turtle or the loon. The animal watches over and protects the clan.

Algonquin people do not believe in land ownership. Instead, they believe the Creator and Mother Earth gave them the land in trust. It is important that the land, water, air, animals, and plants be cared for. Algonquin families are careful not to overhunt the land.

When family members die, they are buried in their best clothes. Favorite objects and tobacco are placed in graves lined with bark and covered with earth.

Algonquin women and girls commonly wore their hair in braids.

CHAPTER 8

Children

Algonquin children had important responsibilities. They did chores to help the family. These included gathering food, water, and firewood. They also helped make clothing, cook meals, and clean their home.

Anishinabek children learned many important traditions. These included the Seven Grandfather Teachings. The Seven Grandfather Teachings are Love, Honesty, Truth, Respect, Bravery, Humility, and Wisdom. These values guided Algonquin in their daily lives.

In addition to helping their families with chores, Algonquin children also had lots of time to play!

CHAPTER 9

Traditions

The Algonquin believed in a supreme being, known as the Great Spirit. The Great Spirit was worshipped as the Creator of everything.

The Algonquin also told stories about Nanabozho. The stories varied from **clan** to clan. Nanabozho is usually said to be the son of the west wind or the sun. In some stories, he has a brother who is his best friend.

In many stories, Nanabozho acts silly or foolish, but he never hurts others or acts disrespectfully. Nanabozho is known as a **cultural** hero and teacher.

The forest is an important part of many Algonquin traditions.

CHAPTER 10

War

The Algonquin based their relationships with other Native Americans and Europeans on trust and friendship. But the Iroquois attacked the Algonquin in the 1640s. Eventually, the Algonquin defeated the Iroquois.

Algonquin warriors used a bow and arrows, knives, hatchets, or war clubs in surprise **raids** along forest trails or in enemy camps. They also used wooden shields to protect themselves.

Algonquin men often painted their faces before a battle.

CHAPTER II

Contact with Europeans

One of the first Europeans the Algonquin people saw was French explorer Samuel de Champlain in 1608. Starting then, the Algonquin traded furs for European guns, cloth, and axes.

The Algonquin people also entered into many treaties with the British, French, and colonial governments. These treaties were intended to protect the Algonquins' rights to their lands. But despite the treaties, the Algonquin were gradually forced from their homelands.

In some cases, the Algonquin received **reservations** from the Canadian government. But some **bands** had to purchase their own lands back from the government. Also during this time, European settlers spread many diseases to the Algonquin. Many Algonquin died.

Today, most Algonquin live on reservations in Ontario and Quebec, including the Rapid Lake Reserve in Quebec.

CHAPTER 12

Iroquet

Iroquet was an Algonquin chief. He first met Samuel de Champlain in June 1609, near Quebec. The Algonquin and their Huron neighbors made an alliance with the French to make war on the Iroquois.

The next year, Iroquet agreed to take a young French boy to his home. He taught him the Algonquin ways and language. Champlain agreed to take a young Algonquin boy to France with him.

Relations between the French and the Algonquin continued to improve. In 1615, Champlain and some of his soldiers visited the Algonquin homelands. Iroquet continued to lead his tribe for many years.

Samuel de Champlain

CHAPTER 13

The Algonquin Today

Today, the Algonquin are known as the Algonquin Nation. It is part of the greater Anishinabek Nation. About 11,000 Algonquin live in ten recognized Algonquin First Nations in Ontario and Quebec. Many more are spread across Canada and the United States.

Algonquin children are beginning to learn more about their **culture** and language. In some schools, children can relearn the Algonquin language.

The Algonquin also hold **powwows**. These are celebrations of Algonquin culture. The men sing around a big drum called the Grandfather Drum. They sing songs about friendship, travel, hunting, and love. Both men and women dance around the Grandfather Drum.

The Algonquin are especially known for Jingle Dress Dancers. These women wear cotton dresses covered with "jingles" made of hoofs or metal cones. During the dance, the jingles make a sacred sound.

A Jingle Dress Dancer at a powwow in Ontario, Canada.

Glossary

band—a number of persons acting together; a subgroup of a tribe.

breechcloth—a piece of cloth, usually worn by men. It wraps between the legs and around the waist.

cargo—a load of goods.

clan—all the people in a single tribe who claim to be descended from the same first ancestor. Some tribes had clans that were passed on to the children by the mother's family and some by the father's family.

culture—the customs, arts, and tools of a nation or people at a certain time. Something related to culture is cultural.

elder—a person having authority because of age or experience.

inherit—to receive from one's parents or ancestors.

powwow—a ceremony of Native Americans, usually involving feasts, dancing, and performances.

province—a political division of a country.

quill—a large, stiff feather or a sharp spine.

raid—a sudden attack.

reservation—a piece of land set aside by the government for Native Americans to live on.

sapling—a thin, young tree.

tunic—a short, close-fitting garment.

ONLINE RESOURCES

To learn more about the Algonquin, please visit **abdobooklinks.com** or scan this QR code. These links are routinely monitored and updated to provide the most current information available.

Index